Made in United States
Troutdale, OR
04/09/2024

19070426R00070